Essential Physical Science

FORCES AND MOTION

Angela Royston

Chicago, Illinois

To contact Capstone Global Library, please
call 800-747-4992, or visit our web site,
www.capstonepub.com

Edited by Nancy Dickmann, Adam Miller,
    and Diyan Leake
Designed by Victoria Allen
Original illustrations © Capstone Global
    Library Ltd 2014
Illustrated by H L Studios
Picture research by Ruth Blair
Originated by Capstone Global Library Ltd
Printed in China by CTPS

17 16 15 14 13
10 9 8 7 6 5 4 3 2 1

Library of Congress Cataloging-in-Publication Data
Royston, Angela, 1945-
  Forces and motion / Angela Royston.
    pages cm.—(Essential physical science)
  Includes bibliographical references and index.
  ISBN 978-1-4329-8145-7 (hb)—ISBN 978-1-4329-
8155-6 (pb) 1. Motion—Juvenile literature. 2. Force
and energy—Juvenile literature. I. Title.
  QC127.4.R69 2014
  531'.6—dc23   2012051635

Acknowledgments
We would like to thank the following for permission
to reproduce photographs: Alamy pp. 12 (© AC
Images), 16 (© Stephen Markeson), 22 (© Fancy), 36
(© Corbis Bridge), 38 (© Marvin Dembinsky Photo
Associates); Capstone Publishers (© Karon Dubke)
pp. 14, 15, 24, 25, 32, 33; Corbis pp. 5 (© A2942/_
Ingo Wagner/dpa), 39 (© NASA/Roger Ressmeyer),
40 (© Jim Sugar); © Corbis p. 37; Getty Images pp. 8
(Bongarts), 18 (Neil Beckerman), 19 (Photolibrary),
27 (Chad Baker), 29 (Phil Walter), 31 (Reinhard
Dirscherl), 41 (NASA); Shutterstock pp. 4 (© Ahmad
Faizal Yahya), 6 (© iQoncept), 7 (© Jeff Whyte), 9
(© bikeriderlondon), 10 (© bikeriderlondon), 20
(© Maxim Blinkov), 21 (© Poznyakov), 23 (© K. Miri
Photography), 26 (© Alexey U), 30 (© Jan S), 34
(© Patrick Foto), 35 (© mahout), 42 (© Denis
Kuvaev), 43 (© Ahmad Faizal Yahya).

Cover photograph of tandem skydivers reproduced
with permission of Shutterstock (© Atlaspix).

Every effort has been made to contact copyright
holders of material reproduced in this book. Any
omissions will be rectified in subsequent printings
if notice is given to the publisher.

Disclaimer
All the Internet addresses (URLs) given in this book
were valid at the time of going to press. However,
due to the dynamic nature of the Internet, some
addresses may have changed, or sites may have
changed or ceased to exist since publication. While
the author and publisher regret any inconvenience
this may cause readers, no responsibility for any
such changes can be accepted by either the author
or the publisher.

Contents

Eureka moment!

Learn about important discoveries that have brought about further knowledge and understanding.

 DID YOU KNOW?

Discover fascinating facts about forces and motion.

WHAT'S NEXT?

Read about the latest research and advances in essential physical science.

Some words are shown in bold, **like this**. You can find out what they mean by looking in the glossary.

How Do They Make That Move?

A force makes something move or changes the way it moves. When something moves, it changes position. It starts at one place and finishes up somewhere else—or it might come back to the starting point.

A skateboarder reaches the top of the ramp, spins, and lands with his feet still on the skateboard. It takes real skill to do this trick, but he couldn't do it without forces.

DID YOU KNOW?

The word *eureka* is Greek for "I have found it." An ancient Greek named Archimedes said, "Eureka!" when he solved a problem. Archimedes solved many problems, often with the help of forces. In 212 BCE, the Romans attacked his home city, Syracuse, in Sicily. To defend Syracuse, Archimedes built giant **catapults**, which hurled heavy boulders with great force at the Roman ships.

Moving objects

People have invented machines to move objects more easily. Some use muscle power and some use electricity, the force of the wind, or running water. Other forces come into play, too. Without **friction** and **gravity**, things could not slow down or fall. There would be chaos!

Making even a simple movement by themselves is a major triumph for people whose arms are paralyzed. This robotic arm is powered by electricity, but it is controlled by the paralyzed person.

WHAT'S NEXT?

Suppose that a computer could pick up your thoughts and change them into actions. People who are **paralyzed** may soon be helped by just such a computer chip implanted into the brain. The chip will detect thought signals and use them to guide a **robotic** arm.

What Is Motion?

The easiest way to describe a force is by following the way something moves. First, you need to know the object's start position, and then you need to know the position where it ended up. You can then describe the path it took to get to the end position. Some things move in an irregular path, while others move in a fixed pattern.

Fixing your position

To tell someone where you are, you have to describe your position in relation to another object or your surroundings. For example, if you are meeting a friend, you might say, "I'm waiting at the bus stop across the road from school."

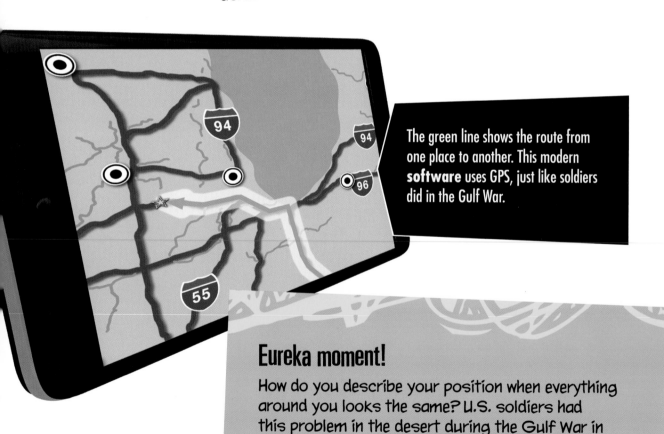

The green line shows the route from one place to another. This modern **software** uses GPS, just like soldiers did in the Gulf War.

Eureka moment!

How do you describe your position when everything around you looks the same? U.S. soldiers had this problem in the desert during the Gulf War in Kuwait in 1991. Then they discovered the solution—a **Global Positioning System (GPS)**. It used satellites in space to pinpoint their exact position. It even worked during sandstorms.

Patterns of movement

Some things move in a fixed pattern. Fairground swing rides move in a circle, but swings on a playground move forward and backward. The parts of a machine may spin or move up and down. Mathematically, a straight line is the shortest distance between two points, but in real life, the quickest route often twists and turns around obstacles.

The swings on this fairground swing ride move around in a circle as it rotates. The swings also move outward and up as the ride moves faster.

Getting going

You cannot move without a force to set you off. All forces either push or pull. You push a shopping cart, although you can also pull it. When you move a heavy table, you either lift it or pull it across the floor. Lifting is a force that pulls upward. The heavier the thing you are lifting, the more force it takes.

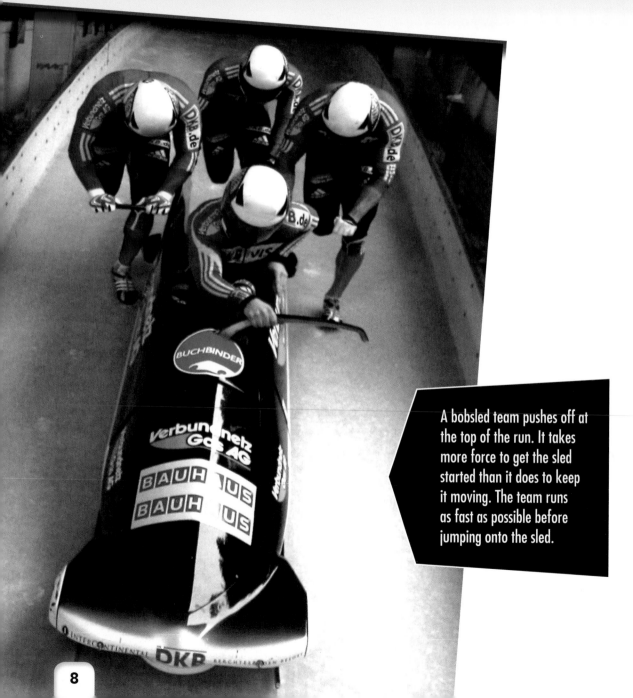

A bobsled team pushes off at the top of the run. It takes more force to get the sled started than it does to keep it moving. The team runs as fast as possible before jumping onto the sled.

Power from afar

Most forces need to make contact. You have to hold a shopping cart before you can pull or push it. Other forces can pull an object without touching it. For example, a magnet pulls steel paper clips toward it without making contact. Gravity is the force that pulls all things down to the ground, whether they are touching the ground or not.

A diver leaps off the high board into the swimming pool. The force that will pull him down is Earth's gravity.

DID YOU KNOW?

Gravity on other planets and moons is stronger or weaker than that on Earth. (To see why, go to page 37.) Gravity on Pluto is much weaker than on Earth. This means that if something fell onto Pluto's surface, it would fall much more slowly than on Earth.

What Happens When Forces Clash?

A force makes a ball or other object move in different ways. It can make it change direction, speed up, or slow down. In ball games, kicking or hitting the ball can change its direction and its speed. Putting a spin on the ball can change the direction the ball takes through the air or after it bounces.

A tennis player changes the direction of a moving ball by hitting it with a racket. If the player hits the ball so that it spins, it changes the path the ball takes.

More than one force

When a ball is hit, kicked, or thrown, several forces act on it at the same time. The force of a kick, for example, pushes the ball forward. Gravity, however, pulls it toward the ground, and the wind may slow it down or speed it up. The speed and direction of the ball is the result of these and other forces combined together.

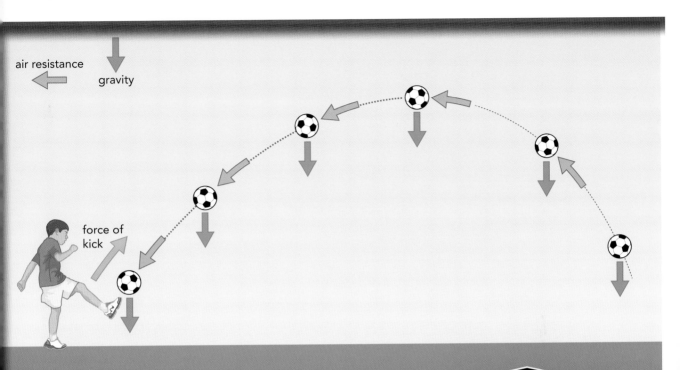

air resistance

gravity

force of kick

Explaining forces

Isaac Newton is one of the most famous scientists of all time. He was fascinated by what made objects change—or not change—the way they were moving. In 1687, he published his Laws of Motion, which explained how forces affect moving objects.

Eureka moment!

What does an object that is not moving have in common with an object that is moving in a straight line at a steady speed? Isaac Newton realized that neither object would change unless another force acted upon it. The **static** object would not move, and the moving object would not change direction or speed.

Balanced or unbalanced?

Just because an object is static, this does not mean that no forces are acting on it. If both teams in a tug-of-war pull with the same force, the forces are balanced, and the rope remains static. Similarly, if the forces acting on a moving object are balanced, the object will keep moving in the same direction and at the same speed. Change only occurs when the forces are unbalanced.

These teams are balanced, and so the rope is not moving. If one team begins to pull more strongly than the other, the rope will move.

Pushing back

When you lean against a brick wall, why don't you fall through it? Newton's third Law of Motion gives the answer. It says that every action has an equal and opposite **reaction**. If the wall pushed back with more force, it would push you away. If it pushed back with less force, you would fall through it. Instead, the wall pushes back with the same force as you, but in the opposite direction.

Bridges

A bridge has to be strong enough to push back against the **weight** of all the traffic moving across it at any time. The simplest kind of bridge is a beam bridge. The more supports a beam bridge has, the longer it can be.

In a beam bridge, the weight of the bridge and the traffic is carried by the supports.

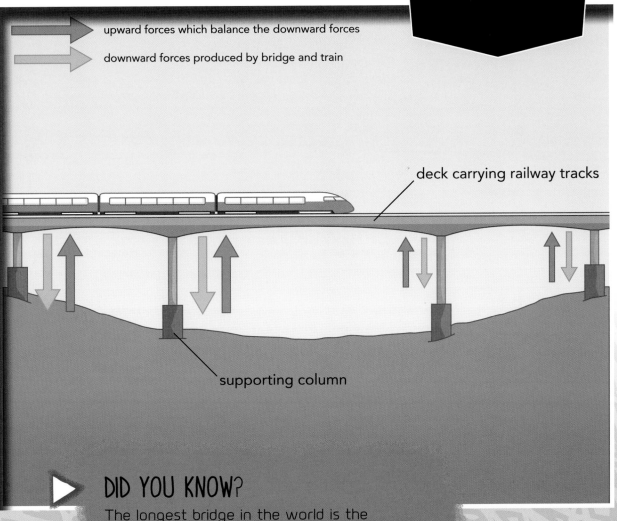

upward forces which balance the downward forces

downward forces produced by bridge and train

deck carrying railway tracks

supporting column

DID YOU KNOW?

The longest bridge in the world is the Danyang-Kunshan Grand Bridge on the railroad line between Shanghai and Nanjing in China. This beam bridge is a staggering 102.4 miles (164.8 kilometers) long and has more than 2,000 supporting pillars.

Try this!

Use marbles to explore how forces make things move. Do you think that increasing the steepness of a ramp will increase or decrease the force with which a rolling marble hits a target?

Prediction

Changing the steepness of a ramp will affect the force of a rolling object.

What you need

- A pile of books about 2½ inches (6 centimeters) high
- A cardboard tube
- A measuring tape or ruler
- A thumbtack
- A large marble
- Five small marbles

What you do

1 Make a pile of books 1 inch (2 centimeters) high and prop the tube against the books. Measure 8 inches (20 centimeters) in front of the end of the tube on the carpet and press in the thumbtack to mark the spot. Place a small marble as a target next to the thumbtack.

2 Put a large marble at the top of the tube and let go. Keep trying until you hit the target head-on. Measure the distance between the small (target) marble and the tack to see how far it rolled. Record your results.

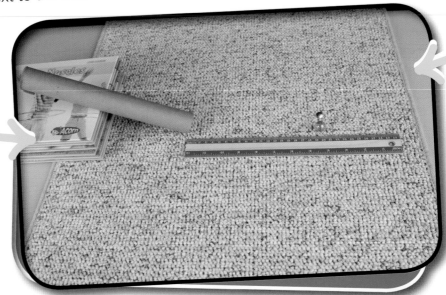

3 Increase the pile of books to 1½ inches (4 centimeters) high. Do you think the target marble will roll farther, the same, or less far this time? To make the test fair, you should try to hit the marble head-on, in the same way as in step 2. Measure how far the target marble rolls and record your result. Was your prediction correct?

4 Increase the pile of books to 2½ inches (6 centimeters) high. How far do you think the target marble will roll this time? Make a graph of the results for the different heights of the pile of books.

Conclusion
As the ramp became steeper, the marble rolled faster and hit the target with greater force. This made the target marble roll farther.

From a small force into a large force

A machine changes a small force into a large force. Some machines are very complicated, but some are so simple you probably don't think of them as machines. A lever is one of the simplest machines. It allows you to lift things that would be much too heavy to lift by yourself.

Pushing down is easier than lifting up or twisting. A lever allows the worker to turn the nut by pushing down the handle of the lever.

WHAT'S NEXT?

When you walk, you use your foot as a lever to push yourself forward. The latest running shoes are designed to help you run faster. As your foot pushes against the ground, the force crushes four **lugs** under the shoe. As you lift your foot, the force stored in the lugs is released, giving you an extra push.

How does a lever work?

A lever turns around a fixed point called the **pivot**. The simplest kind of lever is called a first-class lever. The end of its handle is usually farther from the pivot than the **load**. The small force needed to move the handle down a long way becomes a large force that lifts the load up a short way. The longer the handle, the heavier the load it can lift.

This is how a first-class lever works.

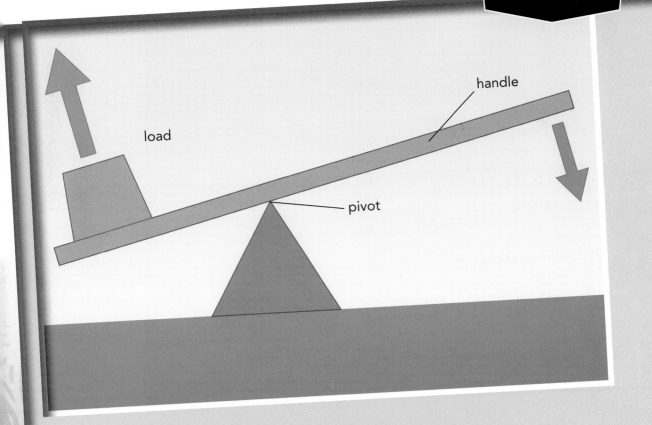

load

handle

pivot

DID YOU KNOW?

Archimedes (see page 4) said, "Give me a lever and somewhere to stand, and I will lift the world." He would have needed somewhere to stand so that he could push down on the lever. Also, he would have needed a very long handle to lift the world!

Why Do Moving Things Slow Down?

If you roll a marble across a flat floor, it soon begins to slow down and stop. Something must be slowing it down—but what? The answer is a force called friction, which occurs when one surface rubs against another. Heavy objects create more friction when they move than lighter ones do.

It might sound as if friction is a nuisance, but we could not manage without it. Without friction, your feet could not grip the ground—they would slip from under you when you tried to walk. Without friction, car brakes would not work.

Imagine a world with no brakes. The only way to stop would be to run into a tree or other fixed object. Luckily, we have friction!

How do brakes use friction?

To stop a bicycle, you have to slow the wheels down and stop them from moving around. Brakes do this by bringing pads into contact with the wheels. This creates friction between the pads and the wheels, which slows down the wheels.

A bicycle brake contains two rubber pads, one on each side of the wheel. When the brake is pulled, the pads rub against the rim of the moving wheel.

brake pad

Eureka moment!

Leonardo da Vinci (1452–1519) was a scientist as well as a famous artist. He discovered that friction is not affected by the size of the surface areas that are in contact with each other. In other words, if you slide a large box across the floor, it won't slow down any faster or slower than a small box of the same weight and material. This is not what most people expect, but it is true for hard surfaces.

Rough and smooth

It is much easier to slide on a smooth surface, such as ice, than on a rough one. This is because smooth surfaces create less friction than rough ones. Engineers often need to reduce friction in machines, because friction wears down the parts that rub together. Friction also produces heat. Rubbing your hands together, for example, warms them up.

A snowboard slides fast down a snowy hillside. The board slides easily because the bottom of the board and the snow are both smooth.

Eureka moment!

Charles-Augustin de Coulomb lived about 250 years ago. He realized it would be useful to know how much friction different materials and surfaces created, so he designed a device called a tribometer to measure friction for different surfaces.

Making surfaces more slippery

Wet surfaces create less friction than dry ones. This can be dangerous if you are walking on a wet floor, but it is useful to engineers who want to reduce friction in machines. Engineers use oil to **lubricate** a machine. The oil coats the moving parts of the machine to make their surfaces more slippery.

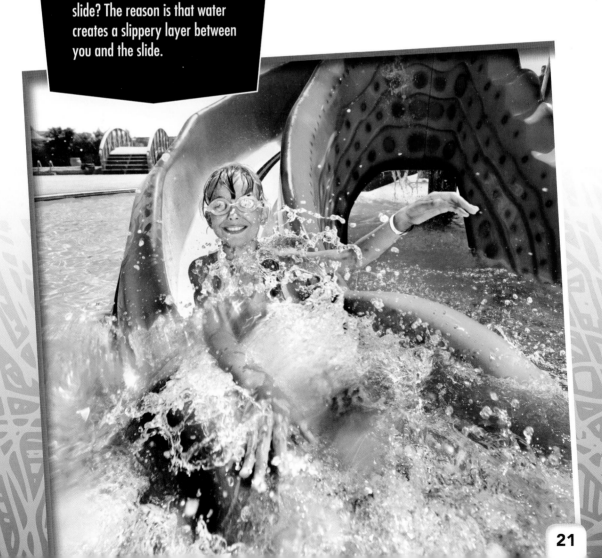

Why can you slide down a water slide faster than down a dry slide? The reason is that water creates a slippery layer between you and the slide.

Get a grip!

How can you avoid slipping on wet ground? One way is to wear boots or shoes with **treads**. Treads are the ridges on the soles of your shoes and on the tires of bicycles, cars, and other vehicles.

The soles of sneakers and boots are made of materials that increase friction. They also have deep treads. The treads push the water out from under the shoe so that they grip better on wet ground. Tap shoes, on the other hand, have smooth metal plates on their soles. The plates reduce friction and allow the dancers to slide their feet across the floor.

Hip-hop dancers wear shoes that grip the floor well. The soles of the shoes stop the dancers from slipping as they make their acrobatic moves.

On the road

The treads on the tires of road vehicles grip the road, but they also slow the vehicles down. Racing cars have smooth tires, so that the riders can drive faster. If it rains, however, the wheels are changed to ones with more tread, to stop them from skidding on the wet road. The treads push away the water between the tires and the road.

The treads on car tires contain complicated patterns. Each pattern helps the car to grip the road in different weather conditions.

WHAT'S NEXT?

A new type of tire has been developed in California. It uses electricity to adjust the depth of tread so that it matches the weather. The tread is fairly shallow on dry roads, but it becomes deep on slush and snow.

Try this!

A spring balance (also called a force meter) measures the size of a force. To do this experiment at home, ask your teacher if you can borrow a spring balance. You will need to find a variety of rough and smooth surfaces.

Prediction

Less force will be needed to move objects across surfaces that create the least friction.

What you need

- A spring balance (also called a force meter)
- A cup
- Several different surfaces, such as a wooden floor, thin carpet, sandpaper, kitchen counter
- Water

What you do:

1 Place the cup on the wooden surface. Attach the spring balance to the cup.

2 Pull the spring balance until the cup just begins to move across the wooden floor. What force does it take? Record the result and the surface.

3 Repeat steps 1 and 2 on each different surface. Record your results for each one.

4 Wipe a small amount of water across the kitchen counter and do the experiment again. Does the wet counter produce more or less friction than when it was dry?

Conclusion
The smoother the surface, the less friction it created, and so the less force was needed to move the cup.

Is Resistance a Drag?

Why is it harder to wade through water than to walk through air? The answer is that water pushes back with more force than air. The force is called **resistance**, or **drag**, and it is a type of friction. Air and other gases also resist movement, but not as much as liquids.

A parachutist appears to dangle in the air. The parachute creates extra air resistance, which allows the parachutist to fall gently to the ground.

Drag can be useful!

Resistance slows down a moving object and, as with friction, this is sometimes useful. Drag makes a parachute or **paraglider** fall more slowly through the air. The bigger the area pushing against the air, the greater the force of resistance.

DID YOU KNOW?

Meteoroids are rocks and dust that fall to Earth from space. Most of them never reach the ground, because they burn up as they fall through the air. These burning fragments are called meteors. The friction between the meteors and the air makes them so hot that they catch fire.

Eureka moment!

In the 1970s, the U.S. space agency NASA wanted a spacecraft that could be used many times. The scientists came up with the **space shuttle**. This spacecraft is launched by rockets, but it returns to Earth like an aircraft. It has no main engine, so only air resistance slows it down as it **glides** back to Earth. At the last minute, parachutes open to reduce its speed as it lands.

A meteor streaks through the sky. It only takes a few seconds for a meteor to burn out.

Streamlined

Air resistance is useful for parachutists, but it is a headache for aircraft designers. Drag slows the aircraft as it flies through the air. This means that the aircraft's engines have to use extra fuel to produce the extra force needed to overcome drag. Vehicles that move fast are specially shaped to reduce air resistance by allowing the air to flow smoothly around them. This is called a **streamlined** shape.

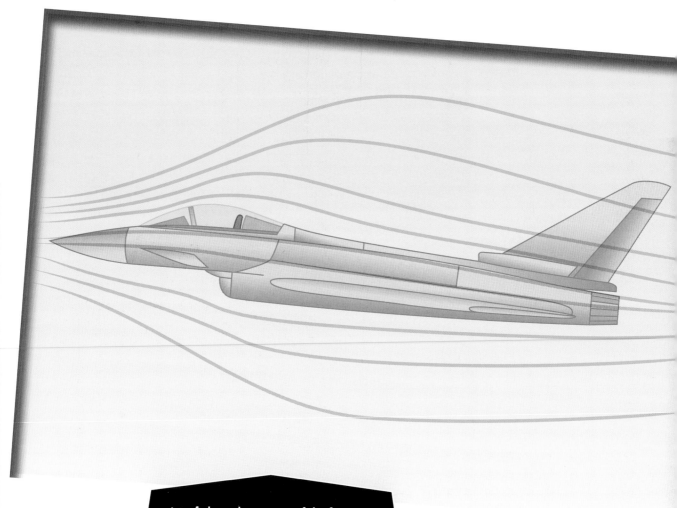

A jet fighter plane is one of the fastest-moving planes. The blue lines show how the air flows smoothly around its streamlined shape.

Improving the design

Designers use various techniques to make airplanes, fast trains, cars, and other vehicles more streamlined. They make sure that the surface pushing against the air is as small as possible—for example, by making the front pointed. They use smooth materials and design the rest of the body so that the air flows smoothly over it. They test out small models in a **wind tunnel**. The wind tunnel mimics the effects of moving through the sky or along a track.

DID YOU KNOW?

Fast-moving animals are streamlined, too. A cheetah is the world's fastest sprinter. With its slim, streamlined body, long tail, long legs, and powerful muscles, it can run at up to 70 miles (110 kilometers) per hour. A peregrine falcon dives onto its prey at an amazing 200 miles (330 kilometers) per hour. It closes its wings to make itself ultrastreamlined.

A cyclist bends low over the handlebars and wears tight clothes. She is making herself more streamlined to reduce air resistance. Her helmet protects her head, but it is also streamlined to reduce drag.

Water resistance

Water resistance is stronger than air resistance because water is **denser**, or thicker, than air. Ships and most boats are streamlined, with a long, slim shape and a pointed bow to help them cut through the water.

Some types of boat reduce water resistance further by rising partly or completely out of the water. The shape of the **hull** of a speedboat makes it rise out of the water as the boat goes faster. Hydrofoils have underwater wings, or foils, that push up through the water, lifting the rest of the craft into the air.

It is thrilling to skim across the water on a speedboat. As the boat's speed increases, the force of the water lifts up the bow.

The fastest swimmers

The fastest sea animals are fish, particularly sailfish, marlin, and swordfish. Their bodies are streamlined and they have a sword-shaped spike that cuts through the water. It is difficult to measure the speed of a fish, but it is thought that a sailfish can swim at 67 miles (108 kilometers) per hour.

The sailfish is the fastest-moving sea animal. It not only swims fast, but it can also leap out of the water and glide through the air for several seconds.

Eureka moment!

In the 1950s, the British engineer Christopher Cockerell invented the **hovercraft.** He realized that a ship would avoid water resistance altogether if it moved over the surface of the water on a cushion of air. He tested his idea by blowing air from a vacuum cleaner through an empty cat food can inside an empty coffee can. The cat food can hovered!

Try this!

Test out a big, medium-sized, and small parachute to find out which has the most air resistance. You will need a friend to help you time how long the parachutes take to reach the ground.

Prediction

The larger the surface area is, the greater its air resistance will be.

What you need

- A large plastic bag
- Scissors and ruler
- Nine pieces of string, each one 8 inches (20 centimeters) long
- Three pieces of string, each one 12 inches (30 centimeters) long
- Three twist ties
- Three "parachutists" (e.g., plastic figures), all identical
- A stopwatch

What you do

1 Cut a piece of plastic 15 × 15 inches (40 × 40 centimeters) square. Use the scissors to make holes at the corners of the square. Thread a 7½-inch (20-centimeter) piece of string through three of the holes and one longer piece of string through the fourth hole. Tie each piece of string in place.

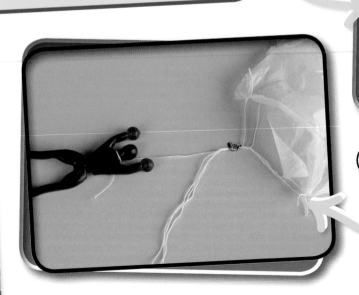

2 Hold the free ends of the strings together and twist the ties around them. Tie the parachutist to the longer piece of string so that it hangs below the parachute. Adjust the strings so that the parachute is balanced.

3 Cut two more pieces of plastic, one 12 × 12 inches (30 × 30 centimeters) and the other 7½ × 7½ inches (20 × 20 centimeters) square. Repeat steps 1 and 2 to make two more parachutes.

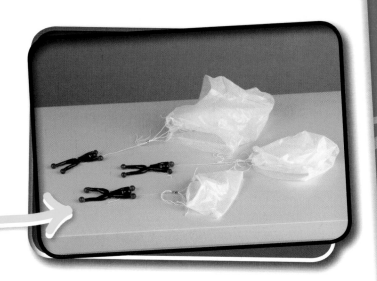

4 Ask your friend to stand on a chair, ready to drop the first parachute. Say, "Go!" and use the stopwatch to time how long it takes for the parachute to drop to the ground.

5 Record the time and then test the other two parachutes in the same way. Make sure you drop each parachute from the same height above the ground.

Conclusion

Which of the three parachutes did you think would take the longest to fall? Was your prediction right?

Gravity: What's It All About?

Earth's gravity pulls everything toward the ground, but Earth is not the only source of gravity. It also exists between any two objects—and the more massive the objects, the stronger the force. Earth is so massive that its force of gravity is the only one we notice as we move around on Earth.

Gravity becomes weaker as objects move apart. Nevertheless, you would have to travel a long way from Earth before you felt any difference. Even 60 miles (100 kilometers) into space, Earth's gravity is only 3 percent less powerful.

When a golf club hits the ball, it pushes the ball upward and forward, but eventually gravity pulls it back down.

A roller coaster uses acceleration (increasing speed) and gravity to give a thrilling ride. At some points, you are pinned to your seat, while at the top you feel weightless.

Eureka moment!

The pull of gravity on heavy objects is stronger than on light objects, so you might expect heavy objects to fall faster than light objects. The Italian scientist Galileo was the first to realize that all objects fall at the same speed. He is said to have dropped a large and small cannonball from the Leaning Tower of Pisa in 1590. They reached the ground at the same time.

DID YOU KNOW?

At some points on a roller-coaster ride, the force that drives the cars can be up to four times stronger than gravity. You feel it when the car climbs fast uphill. At the top, however, the force decreases and exactly balances gravity. Then, the driving force combines with gravity to swoop you downhill.

Gravity and weight

What does gravity have to do with weight? It has everything to do with weight, because weight is a measure of the force of gravity. Gravity increases as **mass** increases. Mass is the amount of **matter** or "stuff" that something contains. A brick has lots of matter closely packed together. It weighs more than a pillow, which contains less matter, even though it takes up more space.

This weight lifter is using the power of his muscles to lift heavy metal weights. To do this, he has to overcome the force of gravity.

Gravity on the Moon

Some planets and most moons have less mass than Earth, and so their gravity is weaker than Earth's gravity. For example, our Moon has one-sixth as much matter as Earth, and so its gravity is one-sixth of that on Earth. If you landed on the Moon, your mass would stay the same, but your weight would drop to one-sixth of that on Earth. The Moon's weak gravity would also mean you could jump six times as high!

An astronaut hops around on a Moon landing. The Moon's gravity is so weak that hopping and leaping take very little effort.

Eureka moment!

Astronaut Alan Shepard enjoyed golfing. When he went to the Moon in 1971, he took a golf club and two balls with him. He realized that the Moon's weak gravity and lack of air meant he could hit the balls farther than anyone had before. No one knows how far the balls actually went, but it was probably over 1 mile (2 kilometers).

Weightless in space

Astronauts in a space station move by pushing themselves off the walls and floating around. Everything else floats, too, unless it is tucked away in a cabinet or stuck in place by Velcro. The space station and everything on board are weightless, but they have not escaped from gravity.

Astronauts on the International Space Station float and turn upside-down in midair. The space station is only 60 miles (100 kilometers) from Earth, so what has happened to gravity?

This astronaut is using an exercise machine in space. Astronauts have to exercise daily to keep their muscles strong.

Floating or falling?

The space station **orbits** Earth once every 90 minutes. It travels at exactly the right speed for it to stay in orbit. If it went any faster, it would zoom off into space. If it went any slower, the force of gravity would pull it down to Earth. Instead, the space station is in a constant state of **free fall** called microgravity. Astronauts feel as if they are floating, but in fact they are falling at exactly the same speed as the space station. Everything else in the space station is in free fall, too.

DID YOU KNOW?

Whenever we move on Earth, our muscles have to work against the force of gravity. In space, muscles hardly need to work at all. If astronauts who stay in space for months at a time did not exercise, they would not even be able to stand up when they got back to Earth.

What holds the universe together?

It was Isaac Newton who realized that the force of gravity (which makes apples fall from trees) is the same force that keeps Earth in orbit around the Sun. The Sun is so massive that its gravity causes all the planets and objects in the solar system to orbit around it.

Mighty or weak?

You might think that gravity is a mighty force. In fact, scientists are surprised that gravity is much weaker than other basic forces, such as electrical force. If it weren't weak, however, the universe would not exist as it is. It would be difficult to move on Earth, and Earth itself would be pulled into the Sun!

This apple tree is in the garden of Isaac Newton's house in Woolsthorpe, England. He is said to have been sitting under a similar tree when an apple fell to the ground and got him thinking about the force of gravity.

The universe

The Sun is a star, and it is one star among billions that form our galaxy, the Milky Way. Gravity controls the movement of all those stars as well as their planets and moons. The power of gravity does not end there. The universe contains billions of galaxies, which are all held together by gravity.

The Hubble Space Telescope took this photograph of some of the billions of stars in the universe.

WHAT'S NEXT?

Scientists are still trying to understand gravity. They have found a tiny **particle**, which they have called the Higgs boson, that may hold the key. Scientists say it explains why particles group together to form objects that have mass. Without mass, there would be no gravity!

Can You Spot the Forces?

You can see the effect of pushes and pulls, friction, resistance, and gravity wherever there is movement or action around you. For example, we can see the incredible skills and strength pole vaulters have, but forces are at work in their feats, too.

A pole vaulter needs to generate a lot of force to overcome gravity and air resistance and propel herself over the high bar. Friction between her feet and the ground allows her to push off strongly without slipping. Friction also allows her to grip the pole in her hands. Air resistance slows her flight, but once she has cleared the jump, gravity pulls her safely back to the ground.

A pole vaulter leaps into the air and uses a long pole to lever herself even higher off the ground.

Skateboarding

Friction and gravity have star roles in skateboarding tricks. The skateboard rolls easily, because its smooth wheels reduce friction. However, the top of the board is rough, which increases friction and allows the skater to grip the board, even in the air. Gravity helps the skateboarder roll faster down the ramp. When he reaches the other side, he jumps and spins, knowing that gravity will pull him down again.

You cannot see the forces that combine to produce a spectacular skateboarding move, but you can see their result.

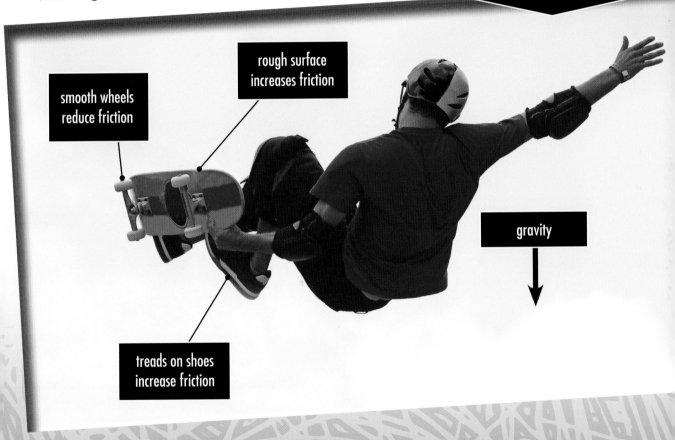

smooth wheels reduce friction

rough surface increases friction

gravity

treads on shoes increase friction

WHAT'S NEXT?

Inventors and engineers work constantly to invent new devices and machines that will improve the way we do things. Who knows what will happen next? One thing's for sure: if a new idea involves movement, it will involve a new way of using and combining forces.

Glossary

catapult machine that throws rocks or other missiles

dense when the particles of which something is composed are packed tightly together

drag *see* resistance

free fall falling due to the force of gravity

friction force produced when one surface moves across or rubs against another

glide fly without moving the wings (bird) or without engines (aircraft)

Global Positioning System (GPS) device that uses signals from satellites in space to pinpoint a position on Earth

gravity force of attraction between two objects, but especially between an object and Earth. On Earth, gravity pulls things down to the ground.

hovercraft vehicle that travels over the surface of the sea or flat land on a cushion of air

hull body of a boat or ship, especially the sides and bottom

load something that has to be lifted or moved

lubricate coat a surface with oil or water to reduce friction

lug part that sticks out

mass amount of matter that an object contains

matter anything that has weight

orbit travel in a fixed path around and around another object in space

paraglider large, inflatable wing that carries a person sitting below it gently through the air

paralyzed unable to move because of damage to the nerves

particle tiny piece of matter

pivot fixed point about which a lever turns

reaction force produced in response to another force

resistance force that slows down or acts against another force

robotic controlled by a computer

software computer program

space shuttle spacecraft that looked like a huge airplane and returned to Earth like a glider

static not moving

streamlined has a smooth shape that reduces air resistance

tread ridge on the soles of shoes or on tires that grip the floor or ground. Treads on tires give more grip on wet roads by pushing the water away and on soft or dusty roads by biting through the loose surface.

weight measure of the force of gravity on a particular object

wind tunnel large tube that mimics the conditions of moving through the air. Engineers use wind tunnels to help them design the most streamlined shape for vehicles, particularly airplanes, cars, motorcycles, and trucks.

Find out more

Books

Biskup, Agnieszka. *The Gripping Truth About Forces and Motion* (Fact Finders: Lol Physical Science). Mankato, Minn.: Capstone, 2013.

Cheshire, Gerard. *Forces and Motion* (Science Essentials—Physics). Mankato, Minn.: Smart Apple Media, 2007.

DeRosa, Tom, and Carolyn Reeves. *Forces and Motion: From High-Speed Jets to Wind-Up Toys* (Investigate the Possibilities). Green Forest, Ark.: Master, 2009.

Sohn, Emily. *A Crash Course in Forces and Motion* (Graphic Science). Mankato, Minn.: Capstone, 2007.

Web sites

www.historyforkids.org/scienceforkids/physics/machines/lever.htm
This web site gives you the history of levers, from the first animals that used them to Archimedes, and explains why they work.

idahoptv.org/dialogue4kids/season9/forcesmotion/facts.cfm
Learn more about forces and motion on this web site.

pbskids.org/sid/funwithfriction.html
PBS offers a game that lets you explore friction on different surfaces.

spaceplace.nasa.gov/what-is-gravity
This is one of NASA's web sites for kids. It tells you how gravity works in space and describes its part in making the universe the way it is.

starchild.gsfc.nasa.gov/docs/StarChild/StarChild.html
NASA's web site for kids includes everything you want to know about space.

Places to visit

Exploratorium
Pier 15
San Francisco, California 94111
www.exploratorium.edu
This museum examines many different aspects of science, including forces and motion, and offers hands-on activities.

Museum of Science and Industry
5700 S. Lake Shore Drive
Chicago, Illinois 60637
www.msichicago.org
This museum includes lots of exhibits relating to forces and motion, including explanations of flight and Newton's Laws of Motion.

Playgrounds, fairgrounds, and theme parks are good places to see swings, carousels, slides, and other examples of forces in action.

Further research

You can explore many aspects of forces and how they affect movement. Go to your local library and look for books or visit a science museum. Here are some suggestions you can research on the Internet.

Go to this web site to find out how astronauts eat, drink, and wash themselves, and learn much more about what it is like to live in a space station: www.nasa.gov/audience/foreducators/teachingfromspace/dayinthelife/index.html

Find out how paragliding works at:
adventure.howstuffworks.com/paragliding.htm

Find out more about how fast animals are streamlined. Search for "fastest animals" and then look for a web site or a book about each animal.

Index